KS1

VISUAL REVISION GUIDE

SUCCESS

English

Author
Lynn Huggins-Cooper

CONTENTS

READING

Revised

- **Amazing Alliteration!** .... 4 ☐
- **Silly Syllables** .... 6 ☐
- **One Potato, Two Potatoes** .... 8 ☐
- **Rhyme Time!** .... 10 ☐
- **Naming Words** .... 12 ☐
- **Verbs and Adverbs** .... 14 ☐
- **Super Spellings!** .... 16 ☐
- **Perfect Punctuation!** .... 18 ☐
- **The Word Snake Game** .... 20 ☐
- **Test Round-up** .... 22 ☐

READING AND WRITING

Revised

- **Getting Started** .... 24 ☐
- **Planning the Plot** .... 26 ☐
- **Super Starters** .... 28 ☐
- **I Say … I Say … I Say!** .... 30 ☐
- **Wonderful Words!** .... 32 ☐
- **Similes and Metaphors!** .... 34 ☐
- **Investigation** .... 36 ☐
- **Test Round-up** .... 38 ☐

2

CONTENTS

WRITING

		Revised
Lovely Letters!	40	☐
More Lovely Letters!	42	☐
Writing Real Life	44	☐
Read All About it!	46	☐
Reading Comprehension	48	☐
Test Round-up	50	☐

TEST, ANSWERS AND GLOSSARY

		Revised
National Test Practice	52	☐
National Test Practice Answers	59	☐
Test Round-up Answers	59	☐
Glossary	63	☐

3

READING

AMAZING ALLITERATION!

WHAT IS ALLITERATION?

Alliteration is where one letter sound is repeated lots of times in a sentence or piece of writing. The author uses it to create an effect.

If you were writing about a snake, for example, you might like to use lots of 'ssss' sounds, so that people reading your writing think about the noise a snake makes!

A sneaky snake slithered silently ...

If you were writing about a fierce bear, you could make your readers think about roaring by repeating a 'rrr' sound:

A ferocious bear rushed around, growling and roaring ...

TONGUE-TWISTERS

Do you know any tongue-twisters? They usually use lots of alliteration — and that's what makes them hard to say! Try saying these tongue-twisting sentences to yourself. Keep repeating them and see how many times you can say them without making a mistake.

Try:

- ◆ Around the rugged rocks the ragged rascal ran!
- ◆ Big bad Betty bought bags and bags of broken biscuits!
- ◆ Pretty Paula poked a prickly porcupine.

4

FUNNY POEMS

Funny poems often use alliteration (and <u>rhyme</u>) to make a funny effect. Read this short poem, then try to make up your own!

Freaky Frances
Likes wild dances.
Saucy Susie
Is very choosy!
Heavenly Hilary
Likes dances that are military
But Mad Marie
Likes to dance with me!

TOP TIP

When you are looking for alliteration in a piece of writing, read it out loud – it is easier to hear the sounds that way.

Bacon butties are brilliant!

Are you using alliteration or ordering breakfast?

QUICK TEST

Which sound is repeated in each of these sentences?

1. Lovely Laura liked licking lollies.
2. Tricky tribes tried tracking troublesome Trevor.
3. Ghastly, gruesome ghosts grabbed Gordon!

HAVE A GO …

Look at headlines in the newspapers. They often use alliteration to make a funny headline. Make your own collection in a scrapbook.

ANSWERS: 1. L 2. Tr 3. G

READING

READING

SILLY SYLLABLES

SYLLABLES

Syllables are chunks of sound that you hear in a word as you say it.

The word cat has one syllable

The word butterfly has three syllables: butt – er – fly

The word monkey has two syllables: mon – key

The word alligator has four syllables: all – i – gat – or

How many syllables are there in your name?

There is one syllable in my name – Sam.

There is only one in Mel too!

6

COUNTING SYLLABLES

A good way to count syllables is to clap them as you say words. Try clapping these words and count the syllables.

Car

Motorbike

Bicycle

Scooter

Helicopter

Aeroplane

TOP TIP
Counting syllables by saying words out loud is easier than trying to count them in your head.

QUICK TEST

Which word in each set has the most syllables?

1. donkey horse cow
2. poppy daffodil rose
3. puppy kitten chinchilla
4. spider ladybird slug

ANSWERS: 1. Donkey 2. Daffodil 3. Chinchilla 4. Ladybird

HAVE A GO ...

Clap and count the syllables in your friends' names.

READING

READING

WHAT DOES PLURAL MEAN?

Plural is a way of describing more than one. When words are changed from meaning one thing (singular) to more than one thing (plural) there are special rules about the way the ending of the word changes.

With most words, we show that there is more than one by adding an -s to the end of the word.

cat → cats   dog → dogs   boy → boys   girl → girls

With words that already end in -s, we sometimes add -es:

bus → buses
loss → losses

ONE POTATO, TWO POTATOES ...

SPECIAL WORDS

There are some special words that change completely when you change from one (singular) to more than one (plural).

mouse → mice   man → men

TOP TIP
You just have to learn these special words like learning spellings. Make some cards with the singular version of a word on one side and the plural on the other. Then test yourself!

8

WORD ENDINGS

Some words have special rules when you change from one (singular) to more than one (plural).

With words that end in -o, you add -es for the plural.

> Potato (one potato) changes to potatoes
> Tomato (one tomato) changes to tomatoes

With words that end in -y, you take away the -y, and add -ies for the plural.

> lady → ladies   pony → ponies

With words that end in -f, you take away the -f, and add -ves for the plural.

> leaf → leaves   loaf → loaves
> calf → calves   wife → wives

This is quite difficult, isn't it?

Yes, but not as difficult as it would be if you changed from singular to plural! One of you is quite enough!

QUICK TEST

Change the words below to show that they have changed from singular (one) to plural (more than one):

1. Baby →
2. Lolly →
3. Bag →
4. Wolf →

ANSWERS: 1. Babies 2. Lollies 3. Bags 4. Wolves

HAVE A GO ...

Play a game with a partner – perhaps an older brother or sister, or your parents. Take turns to say a singular word that your partner has to change to a plural.

READING

RHYME TIME!

WHAT IS A RHYME?

When we talk about words rhyming, we mean they contain the same sound.

These words all rhyme:

Bed and red   Cat and bat
Make and take   Pin and bin
Pet and vet   Pot and dot

TOP TIP
Make a list of words that rhyme in a notebook. Try to find different spellings with the same sound. It's easy once you get in the swing of it!

SAME SOUNDS – DIFFERENT LETTERS!

Words do not need to be spelled in the same way to rhyme. As long as the letters make the same sound, the words rhyme.

Head and bed
Pie and cry
Chair and bear
Floor and more

The letters ee, ea, ie and y can all make the same sound!

10

POETRY AND RHYME

Poetry often, but not always, uses rhyme.

Read the poem below – it is a well-known nursery rhyme.

> H<u>um</u>pty D<u>um</u>pty sat on a w<u>all</u>,
> H<u>um</u>pty D<u>um</u>pty had a great f<u>all</u>!
> All the King's horses and all the King's m<u>en</u>
> Couldn't put Humpty together ag<u>ain</u>!

These words rhyme:

* Humpty and Dumpty
* Wall and fall
* Men and again

Smell rhymes with Mel!

And pram rhymes with Sam!

QUICK TEST

Find the word in each list that is the odd one out – because it does not rhyme with the others. Say them out loud so you can hear the sound each word makes.

1. cat   bat   fit   fat
2. make   cake   late   bake
3. trip   pip   stop   dip

ANSWERS: 1. Fit 2. Late 3. Stop

HAVE A GO ...

Can you think of any words that rhyme with your name?

11

WHAT ARE NOUNS?

Nouns are naming words. The names of people, places, animals and things are all nouns.

Cat, fox, Eleanor, ladybird and London are all nouns.

The cat ran into the garden.
'Cat' and 'garden' are the nouns in the sentence.

The monkey climbed the tree.
'Monkey' and 'tree' are the nouns in the sentence.

Bethany laughed at the joke.
'Bethany' and 'joke' are the nouns in the sentence.

I went to Brighton to play on the pier.
'Brighton' and 'pier' are the nouns in the sentence.

TOP TIP
Sentences always have a noun – try and spot them when you are reading.

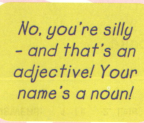
So, I'm a noun?

No, you're silly – and that's an adjective! Your name's a noun!

NAMING WORDS

WHAT ARE ADJECTIVES?

Adjectives are describing words. They describe a noun in a sentence.

The huge spider crawled into the dark corner.

'Huge' is the adjective that describes spider, and 'dark' is the adjective that describes corner.

The sparkling star glittered in the velvet sky.

'Sparkling' is the adjective that describes star, and 'velvet' is the adjective that describes sky.

The brown dog jumped over the wooden fence.

'Brown' is the adjective that describes dog, and 'wooden' is the adjective that describes fence.

QUICK TEST

Which words are nouns and which are adjectives in these sentences?

1. The fat mouse ate the smelly cheese.
2. The stripy bumblebee landed on the yellow flower.
3. The slimy slug ate the juicy leaf.

ANSWERS: 1. Mouse, cheese (n) smelly, fat (adj) 2. Bumblebee, flower (n) stripy, yellow (adj) 3. Slug, leaf (n) slimy, juicy (adj)

HAVE A GO ...

Look at a storybook. Can you find the nouns and adjectives in the sentences?

13

READING

VERBS AND ADVERBS

WHAT ARE VERBS?

Verbs are the words that describe actions.

The girl is playing.

The word 'playing' is the verb.

The dog barked.

The word 'barked' is the verb.

The lion roared.

The word 'roared' is the verb.

The boy is riding his bike.

The word 'riding' is the verb.

I like playing loudly!

Which is very annoying because I like reading quietly.

WHAT ARE ADVERBS?

Adverbs are words that describe verbs.

The girl ran quickly.

The word 'quickly' is the adverb. It describes the verb 'ran', telling us how it was done.

The boy whispered quietly.

The word 'quietly' is the adverb. It describes the verb 'whispered', telling us how it was done.

The cat crept slowly into the barn.

The word 'slowly' is the adverb. It describes the verb 'crept', telling us how it was done.

TOP TIP

Adverbs often (but not always) end in the letters -ly.

QUICK TEST

Which words are the verbs and adverbs in these sentences?

1. The rabbit jumped quickly.
2. The baby cried fiercely.
3. The boy ran quickly.

ANSWERS: 1. Quickly 2. Fiercely 3. Quickly

HAVE A GO …

When you read stories, see if you can find the verbs and adverbs in the sentences.

READING

SUPER SPELLINGS!

LOOK, COVER, WRITE, CHECK

Have you tried this really easy way of learning new spellings? Follow these steps:

1. Look – look at the shape of the word. Does it have any easy-to-remember shapes like double oo in the middle, like 'boot'? Or does it have any tails like the letters p or y? Perhaps it has sticks like d and b?

Baby has a stick at the beginning and a tail at the end.

2. Now cover the word you are trying to learn to spell.

3. Try to write the word – see if you have a picture in your head of the shape of the word.

4. Check the word. Is it right? If it is not, look again. Did you get some of the letters right? Have another go!

My favourite spelling trick is that there's a rat in separate!

Mine is that there's cream in scream!

TOP TIP

To help you to see the shape in your head, write the word you want to learn and draw a line around the outside of it, like a border. This will help you to remember the shape.

16

SPELLING SOUNDS

When you look at words that you are trying to spell, see if you can find the sounds in the words. This will help you, because lots of words use the same sounds.

Big   say 'b – ig'

Pig   say 'p – ig'

Just changing the first letter of 'big' to a 'p' changes it into a different word – 'pig'!

So if you learn that the sound 'ig' is spelled 'i – g', it will help you to spell lots of other words: big   pig   jig   dig   fig   wig

Cat say 'c – at'

Bat say 'b – at'

Just changing the first letter of 'cat' to a 'b' changes it into a different word – 'bat'!

So if you learn that the sound 'at' is spelled 'a – t', it will help you to spell lots of other words: cat   bat   fat   hat   mat   pat

QUICK TEST

How many words can you make by changing the first letter of these words?

1. Had
   (If you work your way through the alphabet from a to z, then the first word you will recognise will be bad, followed by dad...)

2. Bin

3. Fall

ANSWERS: 1. Bad, dad, lad, mad, pad, sad. 2. Din, fin, pin, sin, tin, win. 3. Ball, call, hall, mall, tall, wall.

HAVE A GO …

You can also look for words within words to help you to spell. Then has hen in the middle. Will has ill at the end. That has hat at the end. Mend has end – at the end! Can you think of any other words within words?

READING

READING

CAPITAL LETTERS

Sentences *always begin* with a capital letter.

These are capital letters. Teachers sometimes call them upper case letters.

A B C D E F G H I J K L M N O P Q R S T U V W X Y Z

These are the *same letters* when they are not capitals. Teachers sometimes call them lower case letters.

a b c d e f g h i j k l m n o p q r s t u v w x y z

Capital letters are also used for *names of people and places*.

Sam   Mel   Mrs. Nelson   Mr. Marsh   London
Durham   England   Africa

PERFECT PUNCTUATION!

FULL STOPS

Full stops show *that a sentence is finished*. Most sentences – except questions and exclamations – end with a full stop.

I live on a farm. I have lots of animals including goats and rabbits. Yesterday, one of my horses had a foal. I need to think of a name for the baby horse.

18

? AND !

These punctuation marks are very easy to use. If you ask a question, your sentence does not end with a full stop – it ends with a question mark. If you make an exclamation – like when you shout, or are excited – you use an exclamation mark.

Question marks:

- Do you like cheese on toast?
- What is your name?
- May I have a sweet?

Exclamation marks:

- That's terrible!
- How lovely!
- What a dreadful smell!

TOP TIP

If you are writing and you are not sure if a sentence should end in a question mark, read it out loud. If it sounds like a question, add a question mark!

I like exclamation marks best!

Is that why you always shout in class instead of asking questions?

QUICK TEST

Re-write these sentences using full stops and capital letters.

1. my name is rajan my favourite animals are cats
2. my name is sophie i come from london
3. my name is marie I come from durham i like music

ANSWERS: **1.** My name is Rajan. My favourite animals are cats. **2.** My name is Sophie. I come from London. **3.** My name is Marie. I come from Durham. I like music.

HAVE A GO …

Are these questions or exclamations?
- Do you want a drink
- I love cream cakes
- What's the time, please
- What a rude girl

19

READING

THE WORD SNAKE GAME

WHAT TO DO

Play this game to help you to learn to spell – and have fun at the same time!

1 . Make a set of word cards by writing the following words in dark felt pen on pieces of paper or card cut from old packaging. These are common words that you will meet in the books you are reading.

he	we	it	so	with	he	and	an	him
the	old	big	we	at	been	my	not	if
did	how	where	but	her	then	make	right
could	would	will	went	me	have	can	our
only	over	with	that	she	down	look	because
into	they	off	this	out	now	up	call	in
which	two	for	do	you	all	what	come
get	or	one	here	was	be

2 . Use card or paper and brightly coloured felt pens to make a snake's head. It should be quite big.

20

HOW TO PLAY

1. Lay a word card down so that one end is touching the snake's head. The example below uses the word two.

2. Then you have to find a word that starts with the last letter of the word before. In the example below, the word old has been chosen.

3. Carry on as long as you can, adding words each time that start with the last letter of the word before.

TOP TIP

You can play this game in the car, by playing 'spelling I spy'. Play in the same way – starting the next word with the last letter of the previous word – but you don't need to use cards.

I don't like snakes, they're slimy!

So is jelly, but you like that!

READING

21

READING

TEST ROUND-UP

SECTION 1

1. Match the words to their alliteration partners!

slippery   children

bouncy   dungeon

chattering   balls

dark   slugs

2. How many syllables are there in each of these animals?

Alligator _____   Horse _____

Cat _____   Rabbit _____

Lion _____   Tiger _____

Antelope _____

SECTION 2

3. Change these words from singular to plural:

Dog _____   Mouse _____

Lady _____   Butterfly _____

4. Which of these words rhyme with make?

Cake, paint, take, pipe, bake, land

_____

_____

22

READING

SECTION 3

5. Which words in these sentences are nouns and which are adjectives?

a. The tabby cat leapt into the house through the open window.

nouns _____ adjectives _____

b. The huge slug slithered under the grey stone.

nouns _____ adjectives _____

c. Ellie likes creamy toffees.

noun _____ adjective _____

d. Canada is wonderful. There are lots of massive trees.

nouns _____ adjectives _____

SECTION 4

6. Which of the words in these sentences are verbs and which are adverbs?

a. The fly buzzed noisily.

verb _____ adverb _____

b. The horse galloped quickly.

verb _____ adverb _____

c. The lady walked slowly.

verb _____ adverb _____

d. The elephant marched heavily.

verb _____ adverb _____

23

GETTING STARTED

BRAINSTORMING

When writers are going to write a story, they usually have lots of ideas before they start. They often make notes to help them. One way to make notes is to do a brainstorm.

A brainstorm is just a collection of ideas, jotted down on paper. The ideas do not have to be written in full sentences. Look at this brainstorm of ideas for a story about a naughty goat:

MAPPING IDEAS

Once you have done a brainstorm, you can organise your ideas into the order you want them to appear in your story. You can join your ideas together with arrows to show how the story should be organised – you don't need to write all of your ideas out again!

Look at this ideas map. It doesn't look very tidy, but that doesn't matter! The map is to help you to organise your ideas.

READING AND WRITING

24

PRACTICE MAKES PERFECT!

Try to do lots of brainstorms to get some practice. You can plan non-fiction, such as reports, in the same way. You could also write a brainstorm to plan an article for your school newsletter, if you have one. Remember to tell your teacher about what you are doing!

Here are some ideas for stories for you – you can write a brainstorm and ideas map for these titles – and then write the story!

* The Haunted Castle.
* The Invisible Cat.
* A Horse of My Own.
* The Garden of Secrets.
* Caught in a Trap!

Wow, a haunted castle! Brainstorming is cool!

TOP TIP

When you take your National Tests at school, you will need to plan your story. Learning how to brainstorm will help you!

QUICK TEST

Organise this brainstorm by putting the ideas in the best order to tell the story.
The Magic Crystal

1. A girl finds a crystal
2. Crystal is glowing - pink then black
3. Girl fights evil dragon
4. Girl meets friendly troll who helps her
5. Girl spins through space into different world
6. Troll and girl find a cottage and live there happily forever

ANSWERS: 1, 2, 5, 4, 3, 6

Well, you'll be good at the storming – don't know about the brain bit, though ...!

HAVE A GO ...

Read a storybook. If you had been the author, what important things from the story would have been in your brainstorm?

WRITING A STORY PLAN

At school, you will be given story-planning sheets to help you to organise your ideas for writing. If you also practise planning at home, you will soon be an expert! There are certain things you need to think about whenever you are planning a story.

- **What is your story about?** You can't have a story without a subject!

- **Characters in the story** – all the action has to happen to someone (or something!).

- **An exciting beginning** – to excite the reader and make them want to read more.

- **A strong ending** – so your story doesn't just fizzle out.

- **Lots of action!**

THE IMPORTANT QUESTIONS

The important questions you must ask yourself are: who, where, what, when and why! To help you plan, ask yourself the following questions:

1. **WHO?** Who is going to appear in your story? Are there goodies and baddies?

2. **WHERE?** Where is your story set? Remember to use lots of description! Don't just write 'in a house', but give us more detail so we can see it for ourselves, such as 'in a dark, spooky, old house'.

3. **WHAT?** What action is going to happen in your story?

4. **WHEN?** Set the scene – when does the action happen? Was it a long time ago or perhaps even in the future?

5. **WHY?** Give reasons why things happen in your story. Why do characters act the way they do?

PLANNING THE PLOT

READING AND WRITING

I'm going to plan a story about aliens that try to take over the earth!

TOP TIP
Read as many stories as you can – and think about the story when you watch a programme on television. You may get some ideas for writing your own stories!

HOW READING CAN HELP

When you read stories, make a note of ideas you really like. You could even keep a notebook of ideas. It is not copying – you are not going to write the same story. You are learning about how to write stories and the best way to learn is from other stories.

QUICK TEST

1. What are the five questions you should ask yourself when you are planning a story?
2. How can reading help you to write your own stories?
3. When you are practising your story-planning, what should you think about?

ANSWERS: 1. Who, where, when, what, why. 2. It will give you ideas. 3. Exciting beginning, characters, what happens, description, strong ending.

HAVE A GO ...

Write your own story plan for one of these titles:
- The Terrible Storm
- Things That Go Bump in the Night
- The Enormous Spider
- The Enchanted Teapot

27

READING AND WRITING

SUPER STARTERS

EXCITING DESCRIPTIONS

If a story has a really exciting beginning, the reader will want to read more. If it is boring, people will not want to read the rest of the story. Look at these two story starters.

It was dark. The girl walked down the garden path and saw the bushes rustling.

Crash! Ellie heard a noise from the darkness of the garden. She grabbed a flashlight, and slowly walked down the path. Suddenly, the bushes started rustling!

Which story starter is more interesting? The second story starter is exciting because it has more description, which makes you want to find out what happens next.

EXCITING ENDINGS!

The way your story ends is very important! Try not to end with '... and they went home', or '... then they went home to bed'. Lots of people end their stories this way and you want to be different!

Try to make sure that your reader knows what has happened to the characters in your story at the end. Sometimes people forget to do this. A character pops up in a story and then disappears, because the writer forgets about them in the excitement of writing. That's why story plans are such a good idea (see page 26) – they help you to remember all the good ideas you have as you start to write.

28

WHICH ONE IS YOUR FAVOURITE?

Look at these two story endings. Which one do you prefer?

The noise in the dark garden was not a monster after all!

"I think someone reads too many spooky comics!" laughed Mum as she picked up the tiny hedgehog. The spiky creature had made the bushes rustle and had made the awful snuffling and snorting noises. "Come on, we'll find a warm box for this little fellow. He's too small to stay outside all winter. He can stay in my shed until spring."

Ellie smiled, feeling a bit embarrassed. She had been quite scared – and of a tiny hedgehog! Now she looked forward to helping her Mum care for the little creature until he was big enough to set free, when the warm weather came.

The noise was not a monster. It was a hedgehog. Ellie's Mum put the hedgehog in a box in the shed. Then they all went to bed.

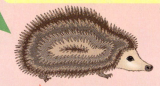

Which ending is more interesting? The first ending is exciting, because it has more action and explains what has happened.

READING AND WRITING

TOP TIP

When you read a comic, think about the last picture in the story. If you wrote the ending in words, could you make it more exciting?

My favourite ending is, '… and then they all cheered Sam and gave him a lifetime's supply of chocolate.'

Ha! 'It was all just a dream' would be more realistic!

QUICK TEST

1. Why is it important to have an exciting story starter?
2. Why are story plans a good idea?

ANSWERS: 1. So people want to read more. 2. To help you to organise your ideas and not forget anything.

HAVE A GO …

Read beginnings and endings carefully. Use any good ideas in your own stories.

29

I SAY... I SAY... I SAY!

SPEECH MARKS

When you are writing and you want to show someone is speaking, you use speech marks: " "

- "I like crisps," said Mum.

Mum actually said the words, so they are put in speech marks.

- Mum told me that she liked crisps.

Mum did not actually say the words, so they are not put in speech marks.

Now I know all about speech marks!

That will come in handy, you're always talking!

ALTERNATIVES FOR SAID

How many ways can you say the word said?

Do not always use said, because it gets boring!

"Hello," said Beth.

"Hello," said Rai.

"Would you like a sweet?" said Beth.

"Yes please," said Rai.

"Strawberry is my favourite," said Beth.

"My favourite is lime," said Rai.

whispered

shouted

yelled

squealed

bellowed

asked

There are lots of ways to say said!

TOP TIP

Remember – speech marks show that someone is actually speaking.

QUICK TEST

Add the speech marks to these sentences:
1. I love rabbits! said Helen.
2. What's your name? asked Tina.
3. My favourite food is pizza, said John.

ANSWERS: 1. "I love rabbits!" said Helen. 2. "What's your name?" asked Tina. 3. "My favourite food is pizza," said John.

HAVE A GO …

Look in books and comics and find all the words for said. Make a note of them – and use them when you write stories.

READING AND WRITING

31

READING AND WRITING

EXCITING DESCRIPTIONS

When you are writing a story, you need to use great descriptions and exciting vocabulary to make your story interesting. You can make a word picture in the head of your readers if your description is exciting enough!

Read these two sentences:

> The cat chased a mouse into the bushes.
>
> The smoky grey cat galloped after the fuzzy mouse, chasing it into the undergrowth.

Both of the sentences mean the same thing – but the second sentence is much more exciting.

WONDERFUL WORDS!

WORD PICTURES

When you are writing a story or a poem, think about the thing you are describing. Try to see the thing in your head – like a photograph. Then describe the thing as though you can see it and tell your reader what it looks like. Use your other senses, too – smell, touch, hearing and taste.

Read this description of strawberries.

> I love ripe, juicy strawberries! They smell sweet, like candyfloss, and they shine like jewels. I love the way they squash in your mouth and all the juice explodes onto your tongue.

Could you picture them in your head?

32

MAKE A WORD COLLECTION!

When you are reading stories or comics – or when you are watching the television – listen for exciting, descriptive words. You could make a collection in a notebook. You may even like to choose words that are good to say!

Start your collection with these:

slime
fizz
sparkle
dazzle
glow

TOP TIP

Read lots of poetry – it often has wonderful descriptions and word pictures, and it will give you some ideas for your own work!

READING AND WRITING

I'm roaring off like a jet plane to buy some mouth-tingling, multicoloured crystals and a plump, juicy jelly frog!

I'll have big pink shrimps and shiny chocolate buttons!

QUICK TEST

Think of words to describe each of these things:

1. Spider
2. Rabbit
3. The sea

ANSWERS: 1. Any, including: black, hairy, scary. 2. Any, including: fluffy, grey, wild. 3. Any, including: rough, sparkling, wild.

HAVE A GO ...

Look at advertisements in magazines. They often have lovely descriptions to make you want to buy the thing they are advertising.

33

READING AND WRITING

WHAT ARE SIMILES?

A simile is a way of describing something by saying it is like something else. You will already use similes when you speak – and not realise it! Have you ever said:

> It's as cold as ice in here!   My garden's like a jungle!

Similes make writing more interesting. They help to make word pictures in the reader's head. Read these examples:

> The sand was like brown sugar, running through my hands.
> The newt was like a bulgy-eyed alien, swimming around the pond.
> The teacher was like a volcano, waiting to erupt.

SIMILES AND METAPHORS!

WHAT IS A METAPHOR?

A metaphor is a way of describing something by saying it actually is something else. It does not mean that the thing you are describing really changes into something else, though!

Metaphors make very strong word pictures in the reader's head. Read these examples:

> The pebble was a jewel, sparkling on the beach.
> The cat was a panther, stalking through the grass.
> The sun was an orange, glowing in the sky.

34

WHICH IS IT?

So how do I know if a description is a simile or a metaphor?

Similes and metaphors do the same thing, so it can be confusing. Try to remember that similes say something is like something else and metaphors say that something is something else.

'The rain was like a waterfall' is a simile, but 'The rain was a waterfall' is a metaphor.

'The sea was like an angry dog, charging up the beach' is a simile, but 'The sea was an angry dog, charging up the beach' is a metaphor.

'The wind was like a lonely ghost, moaning through the windows' is a simile, but 'The wind was a lonely ghost, moaning through the windows' is a metaphor.

Your feet are as smelly as old cheese!

TOP TIP

Similes often describe something as like something else – so look out for the word 'like' to give you a clue. The word 'as' can also be a clue to finding similes: 'My hand was as cold as ice.'

Your feet are rotten old gorgonzola!

QUICK TEST

Which of these descriptions are similes and which are metaphors?

1. The flower was a fairy, dancing in the breeze.
2. The snow was like icing sugar, dusting a cake.
3. The slug was like a rubber toy, sliding across the path.
4. The fly was a fighter plane, dive-bombing my head.

ANSWERS: 1. M 2. S 3. S 4. M

HAVE A GO ...

When you are reading poems, see if you can find any descriptions that are similes or metaphors.

READING AND WRITING

READING AND WRITING

You are going to plan and write a story about a boy and girl on holiday at the seaside, who discover strange goings-on in a spooky old cave …

INVESTIGATION

BRAINSTORM

Brainstorm your ideas:

- Walk – find cave
- Boy and girl on holiday – they would rather have gone somewhere hot and are bored.
- Strange noises, dark – ghosts?

I don't like the sound of that cave…

STORY PLAN

Don't be a baby, it's just a story!

Get your ideas in order!

Who? → What? → Where? → When? → Why?

THE START

Have you thought of a really exciting beginning? What about:

"But I want to go to Florida, not Boring-by-Sea!" shouted Sophie.

OR:

The children peered into the mouth of the cave. Strange, twisted rocks looked like people in the darkness.

THE END

Have you thought of a good ending? What about:

"I think that's as much excitement as anybody needs!" said Luke. The sea glittered and the children walked away along the cliffs.

DESCRIPTIONS

Have you included some great descriptions, such as similes and metaphors? What about:

- The sunlight sparkled on the water like broken glass.
- The gulls circled, crying like lost children.
- The cave was a huge, gaping mouth.

YOUR TURN

Now write your story!

READING AND WRITING

TEST ROUND-UP

SECTION 1

Circle the descriptive words in each sentence.

1. The snail bumbled across the leaf, leaving a trail of sticky slime.

2. The moths danced in the moonlight, fluttering like petals in the darkness.

3. The toad sat on the log like a warty old witch.

4. The cat's eyes glittered like fire.

5. The branches of the tree scratched the window like a monster, waiting to get in.

6. The boy was so excited, he fizzed like a firework.

7. The dog twitched in his sleep, dream-rabbits making his throat rumble like far-away thunder.

8. The swallow twirled around my head, cutting the air with her sharp wings.

SECTION 2

Can you put the speech marks in the right place?

1. I love chocolate, said Helen.
2. Would you like a glass of orange? asked Mr. Stirling.
3. Can I help you? asked the shop assistant.
4. That's mine! shouted Judith.
5. Let's go to the beach, said Lindsay.
6. I'd like a double lolly choc-bomb please, giggled Sunita.

SECTION 3

Write down whether each sentence is a simile or a metaphor.

1. The bat whirled around the cloud of moths like a pilot in a black fighter plane. _____
2. The guinea pig was an eating machine, chomping through the apple. _____
3. The foal's legs were as delicate as fine bone china. _____
4. The spider lurked under the bed, a tiny furry monster hiding in the darkness. _____
5. The butterfly flexed her wings, like a girl trying on a beautiful new dress. _____

WRITING

LOVELY LETTERS!

WRITING LETTERS

Everyone likes getting letters! When the postman brings something for you, it is very exciting. Letters from friends are full of chatty news, but letters from school use very different language.

Letters to friends and family use something called informal language. That just means chatty words, written like you speak them. Postcards and notes to friends are also written using informal language.

TOP TIP
Remember, when you write to friends and close relatives, you can write words exactly as you would say them.

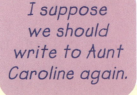

I suppose we should write to Aunt Caroline again.

Yeah, but this time, don't end with 'Yours sincerely'. Last time, she thought you didn't like her any more!

40

AN INFORMAL LETTER TO A FRIEND

This letter is written to a friend, so it uses informal language. See if you can find examples.

> Hi Daisy!
>
> I've just got back from my holidays and guess what? Sprite has had her foal! It's great – so tiny and fragile, you'd think its legs couldn't hold it up! You'll have to come really soon to see it.
>
> Aargh! Back to school next week. We'll be in old Clarkie's class this year. Still – could've been worse, eh?
>
> Talk to you later!
> Love,
> Midge.

You can tell this is an informal letter because:

- It starts with 'Hi!'
- There are lots of exclamation marks, because the writer is excited.
- Words are often used in their shortened versions: don't, you'll, couldn't.
- It ends with 'Love'
- The writer signs using her nickname.

QUICK TEST

Turn these shortened, informal versions of words into the formal version.

Example: Couldn't → could not

1. Don't →
2. Won't →
3. It's →
4. Can't →

ANSWERS: 1. Do not 2. Will not 3. It is 4. Cannot

HAVE A GO ...

Look at postcards and letters from friends to see what informal language looks like.

WRITING

MORE LOVELY LETTERS!

FORMAL LANGUAGE

Letters to people you don't know are written using something called formal language.

That means you do not use shortened versions of words such as 'don't' and you use 'Yours sincerely' instead of 'Love from'. The letters sent home from school to your parents are formal letters. Some invitations also use formal language.

TOP TIP

Look at formal letters, such as letters from school, and make a note of formal language like 'Yours sincerely' so you can recognise it easily.

I've turned over a new leaf – mum's bribing me with chocolate cake!

You must get a lot of formal letters from school as you're so naughty!

42

A FORMAL LETTER

Dear Mrs. May,

We would like to take the opportunity to invite you to this year's Prize Giving Ceremony on 12th September. Joanne has won a prize for Mathematics and we are sure you would like to share in our congratulations.

The ceremony takes place in the Main Hall at 3pm. We hope to see you then.

Yours sincerely,
Mrs. Hunter

You can tell this is formal letter because:

* It starts with 'Dear Mrs …'.
* It does not use shortened versions of words – it says 'we are', not 'we're'.
* It uses formal words like 'ceremony'.
* It ends 'Yours sincerely,' not 'Love'.
* The writer uses her surname to sign the letter.

QUICK TEST

1. Which sentence uses formal language?
   a. We're going to the park.
   b. We are going for a walk in the park.

2. If you were writing to your Grandma, would you end your letter 'Love, Shushi' or 'Yours sincerely, Shushi Sharma'?

Answers: 1. b 2. Love, Shushi

HAVE A GO …

Look at letters you bring home from school. Can you spot the formal language?

WRITING

43

WRITING

WHAT IS NON-FICTION?

Non-fiction is writing that is not imagined or made up. If you wrote an article about your pet for the school paper, it would be non-fiction. Recipes are also non-fiction and so are instructions telling people how to do things.

Non-fiction needs to be planned in a similar way to stories. You need to think about using interesting language, and how you will organise your work. Instructions would be useless if they were not in the right order – and so would recipes!

WRITING REAL LIFE

WRITING INSTRUCTIONS

When you write instructions, you need to think step-by-step what you have got to do. Make notes first to make sure you get things in the right order.

Read these instructions for making a bat-flyer.

1. Fold a piece of paper in half.

2. Draw half a bat shape, starting with the body, on the fold.

3. Cut out the shape.

4. Colour the bat with paints or pens. White correction fluid makes good fangs!

5. Cut a piece of thread and stick one end to the bat.

6. Stick the other end to a straw or stick.

7. Flap your bat!

If the instructions had been in the wrong order, you would not have found it easy to make a bat-flyer!

WRITING A REPORT

Just because a report is non-fiction, it does not mean that it does not have to be planned! You should brainstorm your ideas in the same way as you would for a story. Read the following brainstorm for a report on a school visit to a lighthouse:

- Rockpool ramble
- Stories about rescues and shipwrecks
- Old cannon, nets
- Lighthouse

Now read the report.

Yesterday, we went to St. Mary's Island at Whitley Bay. The first thing we did was climb the 137 steps to the top of the lighthouse and look at the view.

Downstairs, we looked at some amazing displays about wildlife around the island. My favourite bit was the 'pretend rock pool' that showed a close-up view of crabs, fish and anemones.

After lunch, we went outside. The garden was pretty, with special plants that could live by the sea. Mrs. Jacobs told us to feel the rubbery leaves. There was a brilliant cannon and a huge black anchor, where I had my picture taken.

We went on a 'rockpool ramble'. We saw hermit crabs peeping out of shells. I liked the blenny (a fish), because it had big rubbery lips like a clown. We finished the afternoon with some scary stories about shipwrecks. I can't wait to go again!

QUICK TEST

1. Do you need to use descriptions when you write non-fiction?
2. Do you need to plan at all?
3. Is the order of instructions important?

Answers: 1. Yes – to make it interesting. 2. Yes – to get things in the proper order. 3. Yes – or things could go very wrong!

HAVE A GO ...

Write a brainstorm for a report on a school visit, a trip out with your family, or describing your favourite game.

45

WRITING

READ ALL ABOUT IT!

READING COMPREHENSION

Comprehension means *understanding*. When you *do comprehension* at school, it means *you answer questions* to show what you have read.

When you do a *reading comprehension exercise*, you should *read through the passage once* to make sure you understand it. Then *read the questions* and *look for the answers* in the passage. This sounds really hard, but you can make it quite simple by learning a few tricks.

- Skimming
- Looking for key words

TOP TIP
If you don't understand a question in a comprehension test, leave it and answer the others first. When you go back to it, you might know the answer!

I'm important so Sam must be a key word!

There is no Sam in the book I'm reading – thank goodness!

46

SKIMMING AND KEY WORDS

What is skimming and what are key words?

Once you have read the passage through, you will read the questions. Look back at the passage again, skimming through – reading quickly. This will help you to find the right part of the passage to answer your question.

If you look at each question, you should be able to find important or key words.

In the question 'What sort of animal lives in a sett?' the key words are animal and sett, so you would look for these words in the passage:

> 'If you are very lucky and can sit quietly, you may see that most playful, yet fierce of creatures, the badger. Badgers live in their homes, called setts, deep in the woods.'

Once you found the key words sett and creature, you would know you had found the answer to the question: badgers live in setts.

QUICK TEST

1. What are key words?
2. What is skimming?
3. Why should you read a passage through once before you try to answer the questions?

ANSWERS: 1. Important words that help you to find the right part of a passage to answer a question. **2.** Reading quickly. **3.** To help you understand what it is about.

HAVE A GO ...

Remember to:
- read the whole passage
- read the questions
- skim through the passage looking for the answers
- read the passage through again
- check your answers.

47

READING COMPREHENSION

READING

Read about Sprite's foal, then answer the questions.

Sprite is three years old. She lives in a field with her mother, Khola. Khola and her mother are Welsh Cobs, a special breed of horse. Khola is a coloured horse, which means she is white with black and brown patches. She looks just like the horses in old cowboy films on the television! Sprite is white all over, except for a black splash on her face.

Yesterday, Sprite had a baby of her own. He doesn't have a name yet. Sprite's baby looks just like his Grandma! A baby horse is called a foal. The foal feeds on its mother's milk at first, then on grass, hay and horse feed.

QUESTIONS

1. What sort of animal is Sprite?
2. How old is she?
3. What is Sprite's mother called?
4. What markings does a coloured horse have?
5. What is the name of the special breed of horses that Khola, Sprite and the foal belong to?
6. What colour is Sprite?
7. What is a baby horse called?
8. What does a foal eat?

TOP TIP

Remember:
- read the whole passage.
- read the questions.
- skim through the passage looking for the answers.
- read the passage through again and check your answers.

ANSWERS

Did you enjoy reading about Khola and Sprite?
See how many of the answers you got right:

1. A horse.
2. She is three.
3. She is called Khola.
4. White with black and brown patches.
5. They belong to the Welsh Cob breed.
6. White all over, except for a black splash on her face.
7. A foal.
8. Its mother's milk at first, then grass, hay and horse feed.

WRITING

49

WRITING

TEST ROUND-UP

SECTION 1

Write a letter to your friend, telling them about your trip to the zoo. You can make this letter up, about an imaginary trip if you prefer.

Remember:
- Use informal language
- Use interesting descriptions
- Finish your letter with 'Love' or 'Love from'.

Ideas to include:
- Your favourite animal
- Did you see any animals being fed?
- What did you have for lunch?
- Did you buy anything at the shop?

SECTION 2

Write a letter from your mum or dad to your teacher explaining that you would like to take packed lunches to school instead of having school dinners.

Remember:
* Use formal language
* Finish your letter with 'Yours sincerely' rather than 'Love' or 'Love from'

Ideas to include:
* Why you would prefer a packed lunch
* Ask where people eat packed lunches
* Ask if there are any particular things you are not supposed to take. For instance, are you allowed to take cans?

I hope Mum writes us a note about taking packed lunches!

I don't think I could manage one more helping of lumpy custard!

NATIONAL TEST PRACTICE

STORY TASK

1. Read the story starter below, then use it to help you write a story. The story is about a girl from another planet who is marooned on Earth.

> **Story Starter**
>
> The sky was filled with lights, as though showers of stars were falling to Earth. Isobel watched from her bedroom window as the coloured flames lit up the night. Suddenly, down in the garden, she saw something moving. As she looked closer, she realised it was a little girl!

Fill in the brainstorm to help you organise your ideas. Some words have been added to help you get started.

- sparkling yellow eyes
- clever
- scared of cats
- magic
- sparks from her fingers
- odd

52

2. Now write a story plan – remember to ask yourself:

The important questions – who, where, what, when and why!

To help you plan, ask yourself the following questions:

Who? Who is going to appear in your story? Are there goodies and baddies?

Where? Where is your story set? Remember to use lots of descriptions! Not 'in a wood', but 'in a wild, spooky wood'!

What? What action is going to happen in your story?

When? Set the scene – when does the action happen? Was it a long time ago, or even in the future?

Why? Give reasons why things happen in your story. Why do characters act in the way they do?

TOP TIP
Remember – you can collect ideas and special words from books you read to help you to write your story!

WRITING NON-FICTION

1. Writing Instructions

   Think of something you have made, either at home or at school. It could be a model, a game, a piece of artwork – whatever you like! Write down how to make it, so someone else can follow your instructions. It is very important that you put the instructions in the right order, so think carefully!

   Remember to include:
   - What you need
   - What to do

TOP TIP

Look in comics for pages that tell you how to make things. This will help you to write instructions.

2. Writing a Letter

   Write to a friend, telling them about your pets or a pet you would like to have. Remember to use lots of descriptions to make your letter interesting!

   You could include:
   - What your pet looks like.
   - Funny things they do.
   - What you have to do to look after your pet.

3. Make a Book

Choose one of the topics in the list or write about your hobby. Brainstorm what you will include, then look for pictures from magazines to help to illustrate your book. Make the book from pieces of paper stapled or stitched together – ask an adult to help you.

- Animals
- Dragons and dinosaurs
- Machines
- Space
- Insects
- Parties

4. Write a Book Review

Think of a book you have read and enjoyed and write about it. Try to make other people want to read the book!

Remember to write about:
- The characters
- The action
- Are there illustrations?
- Was it a good ending?

I'm going to make a book about aliens!

That's nice – writing about your friends...!

NATIONAL TEST PRACTICE

COMPREHENSION

Read the story about Grendal, the farm cat. Answer the questions in the box. Your answers will help to show if you have understood the story.

Grendal is a huge tabby cat, who lives on a farm. He does lots of strange things and has many adventures.

Grendal lay on the warm stone wall, soaking up the sun. He loved to sit there, watching in the grass for the tiny mice, who lived in the wall. His tail twitched lazily, like a big furry caterpillar. He watched the beautiful peacock butterflies as they sat on the daisies in the garden.

Nearby, Gracie and Sweetpea, the goats, were eating grass. They munched happily in the warm sun.

Suddenly, the goats popped their heads up from their meal, listening to a familiar noise – it was the farmer's car as it drove slowly up the bumpy lane. The goats began to bleat, making excited little noises as they thought about the food the farmer would bring. They loved it when there were slices of old bread in the feed bag.

Grendal heard the car, too. He looked up, then started to stalk up the lane, through the hedge, as though he was hunting. As the farmer slowed down, her car window was open. She saw the goats and stopped the car. She was bending across to pick up a bag of stale bread for Gracie and Sweetpea when she suddenly screamed – sharp claws had dug into her back!

She jumped out of the car, hopping up and down. What had poked her? Then she saw him. Grendal was in the car, with his front paws on the dashboard as he looked out of the front window. He looked just like one of the farmer's dogs, waiting to be taken on a trip out. He had leapt in through the window, using her as a stepping stone!

"Grendal, you are the funniest cat in the world!" laughed the farmer.

Questions:

1. What sort of animal is Grendal?
   _____.

2. Where does he like to sit when it is warm?
   _____.

3. What animals does Grendal look for in the grass?
   _____.

4. Who are Gracie and Sweetpea?
   _____.

5. Why do the goats look up when they are eating the grass?
   _____
   _____.

6. Why does the farmer scream?
   _____
   _____.

7. How had Grendal managed to get into the car?
   _____
   _____.

8. How do you know that the farmer thinks Grendal is funny?
   _____
   _____.

TOP TIP
Remember to read the whole passage through once before you try to answer the questions. Then read the questions very carefully, so that you do not make silly mistakes.

I'd love to be a farmer!

You'd be right at home with farm animals!

NATIONAL TEST PRACTICE

57

SPELLING TEST

You will need a grown-up to help you with this test. Ask them to read the passage to you. Then you should try to spell the words (writing them down) that they tell you. If there are any spellings you find hard, look at pages 16–17 to help you learn them.

Note to grown-ups – the words that need to be written down appear in italics. Read the passage through to your child once, then for a second time, pausing after each spelling to let them write the word.

Ellie ran down the bank to the edge of the pond. *When* she reached the stones, she stopped to take off her shoes. Paddling in the cool water, she *saw* what looked like a tiny dragon peering at her from under a rock. She moved closer to have a *look*. What *could* it be? She *must* find out! Walking slowly, so that she did not scare the creature *away*, she picked up her plastic bucket *from* the stones. With a splash, she caught the tiny creature and put it carefully into her nature *box*.

"Mum – look! A baby dragon!" she called. Her mum came across and peered into the box.

"It's a newt, Ellie. It does look like a dragon, doesn't it! He's lovely. You can tell it's a *boy* from the lovely orange crest on his back. Put it back carefully now, won't *you*?"

Dad showed me a slimy newt once!

No, silly, that was your reflection!

ANSWERS

NATIONAL TEST PRACTICE ANSWERS

Comprehension pages 56–57

1. Grendal is a cat.
2. Grendal likes to sit on the stone wall when it is warm.
3. Grendal looks for mice in the grass.
4. Gracie and Sweetpea are goats.
5. The goats look up because they hear the farmer's car coming.
6. The farmer screams because something pokes her hard in the back.
7. Grendal had jumped into the car through the open window.
8. We know that the farmer thinks Grendal is funny because she laughs and says, "Grendal, you are the funniest cat in the world!"

TEST ROUND-UP ANSWERS

Test round-up – Reading pages 22–23

Section 1

1. Slippery slugs / Bouncy balls / Chattering children / Dark dungeon
2. Alligator = 4   Horse = 1
   Cat = 1   Rabbit = 2
   Lion = 2   Tiger = 2
   Antelope = 3

Section 2

3. Dog – Dogs   Mouse – Mice
   Lady – Ladies   Butterfly – Butterflies
4. Cake, take, bake

ANSWERS

Section 3

5. adjective = a   noun = n

   a. The tabby (a) cat (n) leapt into the house (n) through the open (a) window (n).

   b. The huge (a) slug (n) slithered under the grey (a) stone (n).

   c. Ellie likes creamy (a) toffees (n).

   d. Canada (n) is wonderful (a). There are lots of massive (a) trees (n).

Section 4

6. verbs = v   adverbs = a

   a. The fly buzzed (v) noisily (a).

   b. The horse galloped (v) quickly (a).

   c. The lady walked (v) slowly (a).

   d. The elephant marched (v) heavily (a).

Test round-up – Reading and writing   pages 38–39

Section 1

1. The snail <u>bumbled</u> across the leaf, leaving <u>a trail of sticky slime</u>.

2. The moths <u>danced in the moonlight</u>, <u>fluttering like petals</u> in the darkness.

3. The toad sat on the log like a <u>warty old witch</u>.

4. The cat's eyes <u>glittered like fire</u>.

5. The branches of the tree scratched the window <u>like a monster</u>, <u>waiting to get in</u>.

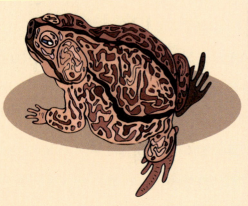

6. The boy was so excited, he <u>fizzed like a firework</u>.

7. The dog twitched in his sleep, dream-rabbits making his throat <u>rumble like far-away thunder</u>.

8. The swallow <u>twirled</u> around my head, <u>cutting the air with her sharp wings</u>.

Section 2

1. "I love chocolate," said Helen.
2. "Would you like a glass of orange?" asked Mr. Stirling.
3. "Can I help you?" asked the shop assistant.
4. "That's mine!" shouted Judith.
5. "Let's go to the beach," said Lindsay.
6. "I'd like a double lolly choc-bomb please," giggled Sunita.

Section 3

1. Simile
2. Metaphor
3. Simile
4. Metaphor
5. Simile

Test round-up – Writing pages 50–51

Section 1

Any letter to a friend is fine. Don't worry too much at this stage about spelling or handwriting, but concentrate on what your letter is about.

Remember:

* Use informal language – you can use isn't, wasn't, can't etc.

* Use interesting descriptions – make word pictures in your friend's head so he or she can see what you are talking about.

* Finish your letter with 'Love' or 'Love from'.

Did you include these ideas?

- Your favourite animal.
- Did you see any animals being fed?
- What did you have for lunch?
- Did you buy anything at the shop?

Section 2

Any letter to school is fine. Don't worry too much at this stage about spelling or handwriting, but concentrate on what your letter is about.

Remember:

* Use formal language – not shortened words such as don't or can't.

* Finish your letter with 'Yours sincerely' rather than 'Love' or 'Love from'.

Did you include:

* Why you would prefer a packed lunch?

* A question about where people eat packed lunches?

* A question about any particular things you are not supposed to take, for example, cans?

GLOSSARY

Adjective A describing word. An adjective describes a noun: The huge (adjective) cat (noun) growled.

Adverb Describes a verb – tells us more. The cat growled (verb) fiercely (adverb).

Alliteration Repeating sounds in a sentence is called alliteration: The slimy slug slithered.

Author A writer – someone who writes stories.

Brainstorm When you jot your first thoughts down on paper it is sometimes called a brainstorm.

Capital letter Upper case letters – used at the beginning of a sentence, for names of places and people.

Exclamation mark A punctuation mark. '!' is used to show an exclamation or someone shouting, such as 'Help!'

Fiction Made-up writing – such as stories.

Formal language Formal language is very 'correct', having no shortened words, slang etc. Formal language is used in official letters.

Full stop A punctuation mark used at the end of a sentence, unless a question mark or exclamation mark has been used instead.

Ideas map An ideas map helps you to organise your ideas, ready for writing a story or report.

Informal language Informal language is casual, using shortened words, slang etc. Informal language is used in letters to friends.

Lower case Lower case letters are small letters – not capitals. abcde… are lower-case letters.

Metaphors A metaphor is a way of describing something by saying it is something else. 'The sun was a lantern, hanging in the sky,' is a metaphor.

GLOSSARY

National Tests See SATs.

Non-fiction Reports, recipes, instructions – any writing that is not imaginary or made-up is non-fiction.

Noun A noun is a naming word – the name for a thing, person or place.

Plural A plural describes more than one.

Punctuation Full stops, capital letters, commas, exclamation marks, question marks, speech marks are all punctuation.

Question mark A punctuation mark. '?' is used to show that a question has been asked.

Rhyme When words rhyme, they share a sound – face/space/race/place/plaice/base all rhyme.

SATs Standard Assessment Tests (also known as National Tests). In the primary school, SATs are carried out at the end of Key Stage One (at age 7) and at the end of Key Stage Two (at age 11). Tests are taken in English, Maths and Science.

Similes Similes are a way of describing things by saying they are like something else. 'The cat sounded like a motorbike as it purred and rumbled,' is a simile.

Singular Singular describes one thing. 'Cat' is the singular, and 'cats' is the plural.

Speech marks Speech marks, " ", are used on either side of a sentence when you want to show that someone is speaking.

Syllables Syllables are chunks of sound in a word. The word Caterpillar has four syllables: cat–er–pill–ar.

Upper case Upper case is another way of saying 'capitals'. ABCDE ... are upper case.

Verb Verbs are doing words – running, climbing, saying .... All actions are verbs.